Ghosts of a Haunted Past/Spirits of a Hopeful Tomorrow

Aphasia Newman

BookLeaf Publishing

Presentation by *BookLeaf Publishing*

Web: www.bookleafpub.com

E-mail: info@bookleafpub.com

ISBN: 9789357740289

First edition 2023

I dedicate this book to both those I love and those I do not. To those I love as evidence that they and I will heal, and to those I don't as evidence that they cannot stop me.

ACKNOWLEDGEMENT

My special thanks to those who've stood by me in spite of it all, even through the hardest of days. To my concert hall of friends, and to my family, chosen and blood.

A special thanks to the following: Echo, Bunny, Kitty, Moonlight, Zero, and Sun. You have been by my side for so long- And I would not have walked this far without you.

PREFACE

In January 2023, I decided to do this 21-day-project on a whim. Poetry and writing out my feelings has always been the most cathartic and healing way of self expression. During the creation of this collection, I was experiencing some dark times. I wanted this to be something to look back on in a year or 10- I will see an improvement. I want the evidence of that. This poetry journey followed me through a mental health collapse, a regrettable decision, and a true decision to go forth and heal. These will be some of the most memorable days of my life- And this gave me the opportunity to memorialize them.

Thank you for joining me on this journey. Whether here by chance or by choice, I appreciate your company. I hope that if you read this collection and see yourself reflected in the pages, you may also find your path to healing as well.

Throughout this work, you may see different sides of me. They are important and deserve to be acknowledged, and I'm thankful to be able to express them.

Funeral Procession

Tonight, the streets of my mind
Will be barren, silent, and vacant
Not a peep from either animal or man
An eerie and haunting silence abound

The first sound to break the silence
Will be the reverberation of me burning,
shredding, and destroying
Every
Single
Remaining memory of you

Then, carefully, I will hunt the version of you
That has haunted me for months
Hidden deep within the recesses
of the parts of myself I hate the most

You may not steal one more minute from me
Your mental eviction notice was served with a
death sentence
There is no forgiveness that you deserve,
And the closest you will get is my dead, dry
apathy.

Nothing good or bad from you will remain

You have no right to any of my space anymore
The next thing to break the silence
Will be a single hearse for the funeral
procession.

Tonight, the version of yourself
You so carefully implanted in me
Will die an unremarkable death
You are absolutely nothing to me anymore.

-ACFMK.

Blood Ties

From the day I was born,
It seems I was destined to
Only be a shadow, only
A time machine to loss.

I was given a name, you know
They say people tend to live up to those
Three names of women revered
I wonder if out of respect, or because they were
feared.

I have always seen myself
As an amalgamation of nostalgia
The recognition for any action of mine
Seems to merely be whether someone else-

The dreaded "someone else"
Whether they would or would not have done
Whatever act of love or service I did
I'm sick of "just likes", "better thans",
and "reminds me of"…

I am not your oracle, nor your window
I threw those names away to shake destiny Not
to have a new one assigned

I do not wish to be a puzzle made of ghosts

-Y.

An Untitled fountain in Seattle

My emotions are like a fountain
They spell over near constantly
Pool up and puddle up on the floor
Cycle on through, cycle on through.
But unlike a fountain, so beautiful and loved
My water spilling out into that puddle
Is nothing to enticing to sit by and watch
Nobody is making any wishes
Or throwing coins into my water.

I can turn it off, is that better for you?
I can leave that fountain empty, is that better for
you?
I can bring my water to where only I can see,
Bucket by bucket, build a new one elsewhere,
Leave this one dirty and dry, is that better for
you?
I can make myself invisible, is that better for
you?

Maybe it was more beautiful when we first met,
When you hadn't seen the fountain yet.

-A.

Sunk cost VS. Investments

Loving another person for myself
Has always been a dedicated task
Never for recognition or reward
But because it is merely my choice

Love, for me, is not just a concept
But a decision I often dwell
I choose to love, and I choose to show it
Each day I must hope I've chosen well

Love, for me, is a dangerous thing to give
It is easy to invest so deeply and someone who
Does not care to return that
And I must fight sunk costs and desperation

The thing about love is that
Even when you move on from someone
They will never return it, like your favorite
hoodie they kept
And I must learn to be okay with that

-S.

Return Policy

It's much easier to scoff and say
When out of love, you never loved anyway
Tell yourself you could care less
To insincerely reduce your stress
What does it matter if they despise me ?
I never cared! I'm so carefree.

…The sad thing about love though,
Is that for any returns, they'll turn and say no.
You will never get the love you give back
And in their mind, no shrine or plaque
Is the love I show all for naught
If the love I've lost is all I got?

There are no returns, nor an exchange
No funerals or burials to arrange
If all we've had is all we've lost
No true assessment to the cost
Tomorrow the cycle will repeat
Because while love hurts, it seems so sweet.

If one day I can't love you anymore,

I don't think I could pretend I never did.

-D.

Chai Tea

8

The sweet tea burns my lips
As I raise it to my mouth
Scalding my tongue as I sip,
Until I can no longer taste it.

Chai used to be my favorite,
But the burn has left me bitter.

I think I'll pour this cup down the drain.

-DF.

Trying again

Another past has come to an end
In spite of all I've lost
I regained you, my familiar friend

Nothing from then can I amend
No ice can I defrost
Another past has come to an end

Many wounds, I can no longer tend
Nor people may I uncross
But I regain you, familiar friend

Regret the letters I did not send
And the ones I chose to toss
Another past has come to an end

No one else whom with I'd rather spend
No matter what the cost
Than to have you back, my familiar friend

There is no way I can pretend
That it does not make me soft
To say another past has come to an end
But I regained you, my familiar friend.

Falling, Stuck, Renewal

"Falling"

Yes,

When I fall, yes, I fall fast
Why must the world punish that?

"Stuck"

Click.

The handcuffs on your wrists lock into place,
I see my own captivity reflected in your face.

"Renewal"

Gone.

There is a version of me out there
I will kill to be born anew right here.

-K

The Bridge Between

Look at you.

You are a beautiful sight,
And so much about you
Is indescribably incredible.

Sometimes from across the river,
I like to watch the way you are-
You seem so sweet and graceful.

There are not enough words
To spell out how scared I am
To ask to bridge the gap between us

One day, I'll have the courage to start building.
-K

Green

Green.
A color that for so long,
We only associated with suffering
And such a painful time that was,
Where it watched us in surround

Green.
Since then, the only thing we give it
Was sunflowers, windows looking over the playground
Toilets, chipped paint, cold linoleum, a sink,
Fear, small, gone, out of body, hands, stop,
please, please, please,

Green.
For years we saw fields and forests
In the same gray you saw films in the 20s
For years, we didn't know why the fog in fallen
No matter how hard, we could not grasp it.

Green.
We never plan to forgive it, not for a moment
But you make it so hard not to.
There is so much that is green about you,

That even as it comes back, we don't flinch so
hard .

Green.
One day, maybe will forgive the sunflowers and
windows too.
You make it easy to remember there is good in
the world
And maybe, that not only bad things can be so
Green.
-K

The Vengeful Child Who Lives in My Heart

There is a vengeful child who lives in my heart.

She stands behind me,
Barely containing her rage
Every slight or small remark
Has her leaning into my ear.
I know her wishes.

I know her wishes all too well.

She whispers into my ear
That everyone is trying to hurt me
That there is no love that does not involve me
Not built to spite me
She is small, bitter, annoying and

She is small, abandoned, afraid, and alone.

There is something she is so very afraid of
She is afraid of being alone, and afraid of being
forgotten
She is 5 and molested, 11 and forgotten, 12 and
groomed,

14 and hospitalized, 15 and heartbroken, 16 and
a runaway, 17 and homeless
She is right behind me and she is angry, she is
loud.

She is right behind me, and she is ignored.

I let go of her little sweaty palms 16 years ago
But she is only getting louder, and I know if I
don't love her
One day, you'll really hear her shine through.
So please, I need your compassion as I introduce
to you

The vengeful child, who lives in my heart
-k

Thirteen Year Old Hands

On my darkest, loneliest days
I look down at my hands
And remember that these hands
Were once thirteen years old

Thirteen years old when they failed algebra tests
Playing with something left on a desk
Or sketching something in the corner of the
sheet
Instead of simply following along

Thirteen years old when they opened chat rooms
And flirted with men for attention and "love"
Begging for someone to see them and love them
Even at thirteen, they needed love too.

Thirteen years old when they downloaded Skype
Thirteen years old when their father couldn't
look at them for three years
Thirteen years old when they brought a blade to
the rest
Thirteen years old when they moved pills to my
mouth

On my darkest, loneliest days

I look down at my hands
And feel those thirteen year old hands
That I wish I could rip out.
-k

Reduction

It must be so hard for you.

You cannot let me have anything.
Every small moment of solace,
You seem to need to taint.
It is one thing to call me obsessed,
But no matter how far I try to run from you,
My legs can never carry me far enough.

You want to make sure
That the ghost touch of your hand
Never leaves my own from moment.
Do you want to talk about obsessive?
You cannot even let my art be my own
Without your spit somehow soaking the page.

What a horrible life you must live!
Having to be so conscious of my existence
Your vengeance is not subtle, nor endearing
And I'm tired of your wrathful spirit.
I did not invite you in here for a good reason,
And I had an even better one for leaving.

My art was made for making bitterness
beautiful.

Not palatable, not respectable but beautiful.
How unfortunate that everything about you
Is so bitter, wretched, and grotesque
That I can't even make you beautiful here.

I know I truly despise you,
But I am trying so hard to forgive you.
Stop creating merely to spite me.
Leave me be as I left you.
Reduce this need to hurt me.
I will not beg you anymore.
-W

500 Years/A Symphony for Something Dying

"500 Years"

With five hundred years under my belt,
You would think I learned a thing or two.
But when I look at your face,
It feels like I've forgotten everything

You made all five hundred years worth it.

"A Symphony For Something Dying"

Butterflies and flowers
Silver rain and haunting melodies
Although the past might be a dark as night,
Because of you, my future is bright
-WXL

Near-Death Euphoria

One day, you will have seen me peaceful.
Nothing will have changed, not me nor you
But I will smile so brightly it'll shock you
I would like to think that this will be the day
That you will finally notice me for the first time.

For the first time you will notice how
My eyes squint when I smile fully
You will notice how my laugh sounds
And how my hair falls when it's washed and
brushed
You will notice my excitement and my joy

You will notice every part of me
That you glanced over for so long
The way I noticed you when I first saw you
Maybe then, you will even notice the bags under
my eyes
But this time, I won't notice you at all

What is cruel decision I will have made
Because in the instant you notice me, I will be
gone.
Now that you have noticed me for the first time
You will notice the void space, it will feel wrong

And you will hate me for it forever.
-D

Do You Remember?

When I was a young child,
My mother told me how anger worked.
She told me that when you are angry,
You will forget every kind thing that
The person you're angry with has ever done

Hearing these words,
I swear on that day that I would be…
Different.
I would remember, I would be different

And moments like these, when I cry out of anger
I almost regret that decision to remember
Because even though I am so, so angry
I can still feel the soft touch of your hand.
-D

Dictionary

I am a dictionary.
I am a dictionary filled with errors
And misspellings,
Poor grammar,
Mistaken definitions,
Mismatched fonts,
It isn't all bad.
Only some.
But I am doomed
To only be defined
By the pages
With typos
In them.
-H

Theatrical Goodbyes

25

The world would be a better place without me in it.

I have known it forever.
-M

The Wet Dark Ground of a Church Lawn

Hello again, Jesus.

It's been a while since we last spoke.
I know I don't believe in you, but
I guess I need someone to talk to
And you're the only one around

Jesus, I'm very angry with you.
People tell me you're always with us,
But as I sit here in front of your home
With blood dripping down my wrist, I still can't
find you.

Jesus, are you listening still?
My blood is staining your ground
As my hands are clasped in prayer,
I still feel you nowhere near.

Jesus, they say you're working mysterious ways,
But I'm starting to think you quit on me.
Perhaps you led me here with a purpose,
A performance of torment, when peace gets
boring.

Jesus, I guess I'm over it.
My arms are bandaged, and I'm not dying
anymore.
Thanks so much for chatting,
But I'm still very fucking mad, you know.
-NF

Keep it Down!

Healing will not be linear,
And today, I threw up everything I ate.
But still,
I think I'm a little better than yesterday
The wounds will itch a bit, I'm sure
But that only means
They're healing.
-KK

Near-Death Regret

They did not see me peaceful.
Instead, they saw me wrathful,
And then they almost never saw me at all.
But, in spite of the circumstances
I realized they had seen me in the first place
When I thought I was already a ghost.
It seems I'm not quite finished here,
And for once, I truly am thankful
Because when I look at all of them,

I realize I don't want to go after all.
-KK

9 789357 740289